PARTNERSHIP IN ACTION

PROFILES OF MEMBER ORGANISATIONS OF
PARinAc - TANZANIA

Mkuki na Nyota Publishers
P.O. BOX 4246, Dar es Salaam, Tanzania

Published for:
United Nations High Commissioner for Refugees
P.O. Box 2666, Dar es Salaam, Tanzania by

Mkuki na Nyota Publishers
P.O. Box 4246, Dar es Salaam, Tanzania.

ISBN 9987-686-31-1

Table of Contents

FOREWORD

In Tanzania, PARinAC is a forum for UNHCR and its national non-governmental organisation (NGO)implementing partners to further operational partnership by sharing information, discussing issues of common interest, review and devising ways of moving the refugee assistance programme forward on a regular basis. Tanzania continues to host Africa's largest concentration of refugees, totalling almost a million persons, and the Tanzania refugee operation truly demonstrates this partnership in action, which plays a leading and effective role in the Refugee Assistance Programme.

The forum has grown in strength year after year. In 1994 there were only four national NGOs in the Refugee Assistance Programme in Tanzania, but a decade later, the number has grown to nine NGOs covering every sector activity in the programme with a total budget of US$ 5.4 million.

The national NGOs in the PARinAC forum in Tanzania have been a great success and demonstrated that, with targeted capacity building assistance, these implementing agencies are able to rival their international colleagues. They have co-operated and teamed up with the international NGOs in taking over some activities previously performed by the latter in the refugee programme.

The PARinAC forum in Tanzania boasts of nine disciplined, focused and committed NGOs which have succeeded in moving the programme forward. They have excelled in their various sectors of operations and proved to be good managers of resources put at their disposal, in programme delivery, management and accountability. They have played a meaningful and effective advocacy role, thereby creating a conducive atmosphere for the delivery of the refugee assistance programme in Tanzania vis-à-vis the public and the government counterparts.

The PARinAC forum is furthermore a conduit where UNHCR strengthens its response capacity, and the forum members also serve as an effective early warning element for our operations, as well as that of other humanitarian actors and states.

One of the strategic aims of the PARinAC forum in Tanzania is not only to focus on the emergency refugee operations but also to play a vital role in the reintegration/rehabilitation after the refugees have gone home, so that we don't become victims of "ploughing the field and forgetting the seed." The forum members have prepared themselves to effectively bridge the gap between relief and development for the benefit of the local population of the refugee affected areas.

This booklet introduces these partners to the wider public and all international players and describes the role they are playing in the UNHCR refugee assistance programme. The booklet should also serve to recommend these NGOs to sectors or players who may need their services now or in future. UNHCR is indeed proud of them.

Let us keep the partnership flame burning!!

Chrysantus Ache
Representative
UNHCR Tanzania

1. Introduction

Faced with the challenges of the increasing number of Refugees and Internally Displaced Persons (IDPs) world-wide, and the involvement of increased number of Non-Governmental Organisations (NGOs) which provided humanitarian services, there arose a need to establish a mechanism with which to facilitate effective partnerships between the United Nations High Commissioner for Refugees (UNHCR) and NGOs.

In 1994, at the invitation of International Council of Voluntary Agencies (ICVA); UNHCR and National NGOs from different countries held a meeting in Oslo, Norway, during which, Partnership in Action (PARinAc) was initiated.

The Oslo meeting defined PARinAc as *"...every activity in which UNHCR and NGOs are involved together. It encompasses all NGOs, which have interest in Refugees. PARinAc, regardless of whether it is referred to as such, is an important part in all protection and relief activities be it in emergency response, care and maintenance or in pursuit of solutions. The solutions include repatriation, local settlement or resettlement in a third country. It is also an important part of our relationship with those NGOs which are primarily concerned with advocacy - either directly on behalf of refugees or as a part of broader human right focus."*

The responsibility of PARinAc is to improve the quality of services that refugees get; improve the capacity of NGOs; and strengthen the effectiveness of partnerships between the UNHCR and NGOs.

Following the Oslo meeting, regional meetings were conducted to establish the PARinAc process at regional levels. Hence, from 9 to 13 November, 1998, a meeting was conducted in Addis Ababa, Ethiopia, comprising the UNHCR, National and Regional NGOs from seven East and Horn of Africa Countries namely: Djibouti, Ethiopia, Kenya, Somalia. Sudan, Tanzania and Uganda. However, Eritrea did not attend. The Addis meeting focused on mechanisms for implementing partnerships with regard to specific areas as follows: Protection; IDP's and Refugee emergencies; and the development of National NGO capacity in the areas of relief, rehabilitation and development.

Tanzania conducted a meeting of NGOs that meet to the criteria of PARinAC membership. The meeting took place in Mwanza from 17 to 18 August, 1999, and it was this meeting which introduced the PARinAC process in Tanzania.

At its second meeting, PARinAC-Tanzania decided to prepare a document containing profiles of the involved NGOs to show the scope of field experience that they have in serving the refugees. This would serve as an assessment of the National NGOs and UNHCR partners' capacity available in dealing with the problem. It would also identify areas that do not receive enough attention thereby attracting other NGOs interested in. This would ensure availability of adequate capacity to respond to needs in relief, rehabilitation and development.

2. The following are objectives of the document:

1. To give a detailed profile of NGOs in Refugee activities in Tanzania.

2. To provide a source of information to all sections of the public interested in National NGOs working in the Tanzanian Refugee Programmes.

3. To provide a point of reference for the international agencies wishing to contribute to the Tanzanian Refugee Programmes and other related emergency programmes in Tanzania and the Great Lakes Region.

4. To highlight the experience and potentials of the National NGOs in PARinAC in dealing with post refugee situations and development programmes.

Member NGOs of PARinAC-Tanzania

No	Names of NGOs	Abbreviation
1	Assist Road Foundation	AROF
2	CARITAS Kigoma	CARITAS Kigoma
3	Relief to Development Society	REDESO
4	Samaritan Enterprise Keepers Organisation	SEKO
5	Southern Africa Extension Unit	SAEU
6	Tanzania Red Cross Society	TRCS
7	Tanzania Water and Environmental Sanitation	TWESA
8	Chama cha Uzazi na Malezi Bora Tanzania	UMATI
9	World Vision Tanzania	WVT

ASSIST ROADS FOUNDATION (AROF)

Address:
P.O. Box 346, Kasulu, Kigoma, Tanzania
Tel: 255 0282810090 Fax: 255 0282810399
E-mail: arofksl@africaonline.co.tz

Contact Person:
Michael Mwombeki, Programme Co-ordinator.

1. Background

AROF was formed in 1997 as a non-governmental and non-profit organisation. Its registration certificate is No. So 9276.

Members of AROF include former employees of the Save the Children Fund - UK (SCF), which was involved in road works and community services as a partner of the United Nations High Commissioner for Refugee (UNHCR) during Karagwe Refugee Assistance Programme in 1996.

A few days after the repatriation of Rwandese refugees in December 1996, the Community Services Section was closed, while the Civil Engineering Section continued.

After the formation of AROF in 1997, it was not until late in 1998 when it was registered. Then, SCF teamed up with AROF in order to facilitate the smooth hand over to the latter of whatever belonged to SCF.

SCF donated all light vehicles, office equipment, furniture, start-up funds and everything else that belonged to SCF to AROF. Thereafter, AROF took over from where SCF left.

2. Mission Statement

AROF works to promote better infrastructure for both the refugees and the local community.

Working in a developing country, we strive towards globalisation, which will only be possible if the rural poor are properly integrated and connected to the global market. This cannot be realised without the existence of good communication systems, of which an all-weather road network is a key input. We advocate for good roads, which are the key elements in poverty alleviation, structural change and modernisation.

3. Organisational Structure

The organisational structure was set up and decided upon by the General Meeting that approved the constitution. Officials of the organisation include: the Chairman, the Secretary General, the Treasurer and Members of the Management Board. Elections of office bearers are held every two years.

4. Staffing

The organisation is well staffed with engineering, management and accounts personnel. There is also a reserve team of temporary staff who are usually called upon to assist in some of the irregular assignments. These are located in and outside the Country.

Nevertheless, on job training and other courses especially in management and road construction are greatly required for strengthening the capacity of the organisation.

5. Field Experience

AROF is well experienced in machine and labour based road construction and maintenance techniques. These include the structural works such as construction of bridges and culvert making and installations etc. Having skills in emergency preparedness, we serve as a natural link between the emergency situations to the long-term sustainable development project, which are within the national policy and objective.

AROF is currently an implementing partner of UNHCR. It manages a multi-million dollar worth heavy plant and equipment unit, which is deployed in road construction and maintenance in Kigoma Refugee Assistance Programmes.

Evidence of AROF's work is extensively documented and is shown further by the good roads and structural construction works that have been done in Kigoma region.

Such works include the construction of Kikurula Ranch Bridge, the construction of 10 multi-culvert bridges along the rural feeder roads of Kagutu, Rwamugurusi and Omukishamba villages and the road network, which was serving the UNHCR Refugee Assistance Programme in Karagwe district.

Also in Karagwe district, the Irish Embassy in Dar Es Salaam funded the improvement of Nyakayanja - Lukale - Ihembe access road, which was implemented by AROF.

By using the cast-in-situ technique, AROF installed numerous culverts along the Kashozi - Rubafu road and Kigarama - Bukwali road in Bukoba District and along Rushwa - Mbunda road in Muleba District.

AROF was involved in the project design of 1750 km road

maintenance of Kagera Road Maintenance (KAROM), which was SCF's last assignment in Kagera Region. In the design of this project which was funded by the European Union (EU) and the government of the Netherlands, AROF did the road condition survey and inventory; preparation of strip maps, bills of quantities, traffic counts and flows assessment.

Moreover, AROF participated in the design and needs assessment mission prior to the establishment of the Kitali Refugee Camp in Biharamulo District. During implementation, AROF teamed up with Norwegian People's Aid (NPA) in the construction of one bridge and the installation of culverts along all camp roads.

In the facilitation of fire wood harvesting and transportation to refugee camps, AROF collaborated with Relief to Development Society (REDESO) in the improvement of Murusagamba Road in Ngara district.

In conjunction with Tanzania Red Cross Society (TRCS), AROF installed culvert bridges along Lukole A and B refugee camps in Ngara district.

Among UNHCR's major assignments, AROF constructed the 12.6-meter span Kahambwe Bridge in Kibondo district. This bridge was designed, partly funded and supervised by TANROAD Kigoma. Also funded by UNHCR, AROF constructed bridges across Ruguzye stream in Kibondo district and two bridges at Muyovosi Refugee Camp in Kasulu district.

6. Sources of Funds

AROF is currently funded by UNHCR in the Refugee Assistance Programme.

Fund raising for road repairs and maintenance in the refugee-affected areas has been started.

7. Future Plans

Since its inception of the in 1997, AROF has been doing road works in refugee and non- refugee programmes. Being equipped with labours and machine based road contraction and maintenance methods, AROF is engaged and will continue to work towards the improvement of infrastructure in the refugee assistance operations as well as among the rural local communities.

CATHOLIC DIOCESE OF KIGOMA
CARITAS - KIGOMA

P. O. Box 661, Caritas, Kigoma Tanzania
Tel: 255-028 280695-2803757/9
Telex: 255-028-2803758/2802043
E-mail: Caritas-KGM@maf.org

Contact Person
His Excellency the Bishop of the Catholic Diocese of Kigoma.

1. Background

Caritas Kigoma is a "relief and development" organisation of the Catholic Diocese of Kigoma established in November 1995, in the aftermath of the 1993 Burundi refugee influx. The target groups of Caritas Kigoma include people of all denominations.

Activities carried out focus on two main areas, that is, assistance to refugees and development work mainly in the refugee affected areas.

In its refugee work, Caritas Kigoma provides:

(a) Humanitarian assistance to incoming refugees at the entry points;

(b) Assistance to refugees in refugee camps in the field of social-pastoral work and community mobilisation; and

(c) Humanitarian assistance to returning refugees who are not under UNHCR's mandate.

In its development work, due to the effects of the presence of Refugees in Kigoma, Caritas Kigoma assists in bringing about development by educating, training, and providing material support to the local communities.

2. Mission Statement

Caritas Kigoma seeks:

• to promote local capacities in the region by working with individuals and institutions especially CBO's in order to create mechanisms to work on particular and current concerns in the region; and

• to give humanitarian assistance to needy people particularly refugees.

3. Organisation and Management

Caritas Kigoma is headed by an Executive Secretary, who is responsible to the Caritas Board. The board has twenty-three members including representatives of the four Deaneries that make up the Catholic Diocese of Kigoma, namely, Kigoma, Kasulu, Muhinda and Kibondo. At district level, Caritas activities are under the supervision of District Development and Emergency Coordinators. There are sub-offices in Kasulu and Kibondo districts. At the village level, Caritas Kigoma works through parishes and deaneries. The Bishop is the Chairman of the Board, which is a policy, making body.

CORDAID (A Dutch Catholic Relief and Development Organisation) supports the organisation on a regular basis.

4. Field Experience

Caritas plays the role of both an enabler and facilitator to the local people in their development efforts in the improvement of infrastructure, and direct services to the local community.

Improvement of infrastructure includes construction of roads and bridges, and provision of materials for construction of school and health facilities.

Direct services to the community are undertaken in the fields of health, environment, education, small-scale income generating projects; supply of clean and safe water etc.

Sustainability is ensured by community participation through their financial and labour contribution. This follows the work of conscientisation of people done by Caritas.

5. Current Sector Activity

5.1 Refugee

i. Managing 12 way-stations (entry points) where refugees come in, rest; get food, non-food items and medical first aid. Vulnerable individuals are identified and provided with immediate assistance required.

ii. In Kigoma, through Holding (transit) Centres, Caritas manages distribution of food and other non-food items.

iii. Caritas supports social-pastoral work in the camps by providing priests with their requirements and assisting in the construction of churches.

iv. Caritas provides transport assistance to:

a. spontaneous repatriation of refugees who are not in the mandate of UNHCR by:

- identifying, verifying and registering the returnees;
- identifying medical needs in co-operation with IRC;
- providing food and non-food items;
- providing transport to their home country; and
- contacting Caritas offices in the concerned countries to receive the returnees.

  b. displaced Congolese in Congo to their places of origin as in 1997/8.

v. Providing assistance to the dioceses of the countries concerned in receiving and assisting the returnees, for example, providing transport, food, clothing, medical care, maize seeds, agricultural tools and inputs for rehabilitation purposes.

5.2 Development Work in the Local Community

i. Health and Environmental Education (PHC): Caritas trains and mobilises the community to improve their health and environment through construction of well ventilated houses, to build and use VIP toilets, and to ensure proper and clean environment. Establishment of tree nurseries and planting is encouraged in the community.

ii. Small Scale Projects: providing professional and technical advice to economic groups of women, youths and disabled persons.

iii. Assistance to local efforts in development activities: in improving the infrastructure (roads and bridges) and provision of adequate, clean and safe water.

iv. In education: Caritas provides building materials for construction of day-care centres; pays school fees for girls and boys whose parents cannot afford it; runs kindergarten and primary schools.

v. In agricultural and fishing activities: provides agricultural inputs such as seeds and fertilisers, etc., and training and advisory services.

6. Caritas' Future Operational Activities

Though Caritas is working in all three districts of Kigoma region, it still does not cover the whole population. Future plans include:

- Consolidate its activities by completing the unfinished projects.
- Expand its development work to cover a larger population. This will include other unattended groups such as orphans, street children, the disabled and school dropouts girls and those unable to pursue secondary education due to financial constraints. Youths as well as women will also be covered.

Credit schemes for income generating groups will continue to be supported. Caritas will continue paying attention to the question of sustainability of projects it supports, through community involvement and participation.

7. Sources of Funds

Activities of Caritas Kigoma are financed through:

i. Beneficiaries such as villagers (and target groups) who contribute at least 25 per cent of capital cost and labour in all development activities.

ii. Donors:

    a. Caritas International Network: CORDAID (Dutch Catholic Organisation for Relief and Development), CRS, Caritas Germany, Caritas Spain and Cafod for refugee preparedness and assistance to development work.

    b. CORDAID as the lead funding agency.

    c. Misereor (Germany) for development work.

    d. Memisa (Holland) for health work; both structural assistance and assistance to refugee work.

    e. UNHCR for part of refugee activities: Caritas Kigoma is the implementing partner of UNHCR.

8. Requirements for Capacity Building

As mentioned above, the activities of Caritas Kigoma are mainly financed by external sources. There is need for Caritas Kigoma to re-examine its financing structure and sources because of two main reasons: first, the amount raised is insufficient to meet the requirements; second, a high level of dependency makes Caritas and other NGOs vulnerable since over-dependency on aid may seriously affect their performance. One suggestion is to look into the possibility of diversifying sources of funds. In addition to its current donors, Caritas ought to look for other funding agencies both national and international organisations. Self-financing activities ought to be another additional source of funds for Caritas Kigoma.

Caritas Kigoma has to build and maintain good working relations with donors, the government, national as well as international organisations, individuals and the beneficiaries as well. This can be achieved through accountability and transparency, creating good public image and good information flow.

RELIEF TO DEVELOPMENT SOCIETY (REDESO)

Head Office:
P.O. Box 2621 Dar es Salaam
Tel: 255 022 2666725, Fax:255 022 2666290
E-mail: redeso-hq@africaonline.co.tz

Contact Person:
Current Executive Director: Oswald Kasaizi.

1. Background

1.1 Date of Establishment of the Organisation

REDESO was established under the Societies Ordinance Act of 1954 and registered in June 1998, with registration No. SO 9459. Its Head Quarters are in Dar Es Salaam with branch offices in disaster-affected areas.

1.2 Membership and How to Join

Any individual interested in pursuing the organisation's objectives is invited to participate in the organisation's work. However, this will depend on the limit of membership as determined by the organisation. Interested individuals will express their interest by filling in an application form, which will be discussed by the Executive Committee and decided upon by the Annual General Meeting.

Membership of the organisation is of two kinds:

a) Individual members who are either full or associate members; and

b) Group members who are the constituent bodies.

1.3 Constitution: REDESO has a constitution.

2. REDESO's Mission Statement

We strive to bring at least peace of mind to the displaced people and development even to the vulnerable communities.

3. Organisational Structure

Refer to the organisational chart provided at the end of REDESO'S profile.

Total number of staff presently employed is 236.

REDESO has competence in environmental conservation, camp management, water & sanitation and community development.

4. Field Experience

In Refugee Programmes:

- REDESO is implementing environmental management programme in refugee camps and areas surrounding refugee camps (refugee affected local communities) in Ngara, Kibondo and Mkuyu in Kagera, Kigoma and Tanga Regions respectively. This involves nursery establishment, tree planting, forest management and protection, soil and water conservation, environmental education, energy conservation, fuel wood harvesting, trucking and distribution.

- REDESO also implements camp management, water and sanitation in Mkugwa Refugee Camp in Kibondo-Kigoma region. The organisation implements camp management, water, health and sanitation and community services in Mkuyu Refugee Camp, Handeni - Tanga.

Type of Service	Phase	Where	Duration
Camp Management	Care and Maintanance	a) Mkugwa Refugee Camp in Kibondo, Kigoma Region: Refugee with mixed marriages and different nationalities i.e. Rwandese, Burundians and Congolese.	Since 1998 to present
		b) Mkuyu Refugee Camp in Handeni, Tanga Region: Refugee include: Somalis, Kenyans, Madagascans, Ugandans and Sudanese.	January 2001 to present
Water and Sanitation	Care and Maintanance	a) Mkugwa Refugee Camp in Kibondo, Kigoma.	1998 to present
		b) Mkuyu Refugee Camp in Handeni, Tanga.	2001 to present
Community services	Care and Maintanance	Mkuyu Refugee Camp in Handeni, Tanga	2001 to present
Environmental Management - Environmental conservation and rehabilitation; Environmental Education; Environmental assessment		a) Ngara District-Kagera Region: Lukole A&B: Burundians (97,375) and Rwandese (17,649).	1998 to present
		b) Kibondo District i. Mkugwa Refugee Camp with 1,519 refugees, being mixed marriages from Rwanda, Burundi and Congo. ii. Nduta Refugee Camp with 49,325 Burundians refugees iii. Mtendeli Camp with 46,728 Burundian refugees.	1998 to present
		c) Mkuyu Refugee Camp with a total of 3,500 refugees from Somalia, Kenya, Uganda and Madagscar.	2001 to present

Direct Service to Refugees:

Services to Refugee Affected Areas:

- REDESO is implementing both sustainable community development and natural resources management projects in Ngara, Kagera under the Dutch Government and the CAFOD-UK funding. Ngara received massive refugee influx during the 1994 Great Lakes' Genocide. The refugees had had serious negative impacts not only to local communities but also to the environment. So, REDESO is strongly working on the remedy to the environment.
- Interventions include soil and water conservation, food security, nursery establishment, tree planting, home gardening, land use planning, agro-forestry and community mobilisation towards sustainable development.

5. REDESO's other Potential Activities

- Environmental research in refugee and local communities;
- Community mobilization through Participatory Rural Appraisal (PRA) methods.

There is a potential for expansion to local communities in refugee-affected areas and vulnerable communities. Also REDESO has an opportunity to efficiently transform relief services into development programmes. The environment is one of the areas that is mostly affected by refugee influx. However, one of REDESO'S priorities is to venture into development programme with natural resources management and food security related interventions.

6. Future Plans

- Long-term development programmes in refugee affected areas;
- Organisation capacity development;
- Educating the community on disaster preparedness;
- Conducting poverty alleviation programmes;
- HIV/AIDS intervention campaigns; and Food security.

7. Areas of Development

• Lobbying and Advocacy;
• Funds raising for short and long-term programmes; and
• Staff capacity building.

REDESO'S ORGANISATIONAL STRUCTURE

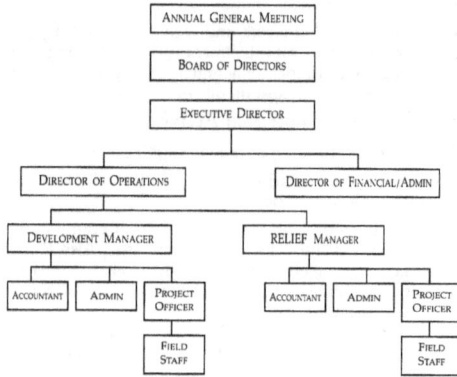

```
                    ANNUAL GENERAL MEETING

                     BOARD OF DIRECTORS

                     EXECUTIVE DIRECTOR

      DIRECTOR OF OPERATIONS          DIRECTOR OF FINANCIAL/ADMIN

      DEVELOPMENT MANAGER                  RELIEF MANAGER

ACCOUNTANT   ADMIN   PROJECT        ACCOUNTANT   ADMIN   PROJECT
                     OFFICER                             OFFICER

                     FIELD                               FIELD
                     STAFF                               STAFF
```

SAMARITAN ENTERPRISE KEEPERS ORGANISATION (SEKO)

Name of Founder:
Bishop Dr. Gerard Mpango
P.O.BOX 13, KASULU, KIGOMA
Tel: +255-28-2810321
E-mail: bpmpango@maf.co.tz, gmpango@hotmail.com

Contact Person:
Stephen S. Kahabi (ADI; B.COM; PGDTM.) Director
P.O.BOX 326 Tel/Fax: +255-28-2810319
Kasulu, Kigoma, Tanzania
E-mail: seko@africaonline.co.tz

1. Background

The SAMARITAN ENTERPRISE KEEPERS ORGANISATION (SEKO) was officially registered on 16th October 2000 under the initiative of Bishop Dr. Gerard Mpango who is its current Executive Chairman. Being a non-governmental organisation, SEKO has its origin in the Refugee Department in the Anglican Church of Tanzania in the Diocese of Western Tanganyika. From April 1997 to 1st July 1999, the Department was under the assistance of the Christian Outreach and Relief Development (CORD). Under a bilateral agreement with the Diocese, CORD was given the mandate of providing capacity building to staff members of the Department. Most members of the staff, who were working within its Community Services Wing in Muyovosi Camp, formed the backbone of this Refugee Department. Since then, and until now, the Department under SEKO, has been providing community services and education to Refugee in the same camp, which currently hosts a population of 37,800 (31st Dec. 2001).

2. SEKO's Vision

SEKO's overall vision is to transform the Local and Refugee Communities in Tanzania from the vices of poverty into the virtues of prosperity so that the smile of hope can shine on the faces of people we serve.

3. SEKO's Mission Statement

SEKO is greatly inspired by the three Christian principles of the Good Samaritan viz. hard work, Compassion and Integrity. Its mission, therefore, is to promote sustainable development through hard work, to respond to relief needs and to show integrity in all of our dealings.

4. Organisational Structure

The organisation is led by an Executive Board, currently with eleven (11) members, under the leadership of Bishop Dr. Gerard Mpango who is its founder and Executive Chairman.

One post has deliberately been left vacant in case there is a request for donor representation on the SEKO's management as a condition to providing financial or material support.

4.1 Daily Management

Daily activities of the organisation are under the DIRECTOR who is responsible for executing SEKO's mission and vision. The Director is also the secretary of the Board and accountable to it. He is also in charge of the day-to-day operations of the organisation and answerable to the Executive Chairman on all activities. In addition, there is a Deputy Director of the organisation who is also the Community Services Co-ordinator. Currently the co-ordinator oversees the refugee programme in ensuring its proper execution. He is also responsible for co-ordinating activities within the camp and for preparing timely reports.

5. Field Experience

The Refugee Programme

The SEKO's Community Services Programme at Muyovosi seeks to help refugees to undergo attitudinal changes in an environment of loving and caring relationships. Through such an approach the refugee community itself will be able to address the social and economic needs of vulnerable and disadvantaged groups within the refugee community. Aims of the programme are to enable community groups and individuals to:

- develop their own solutions to the problems they face;
- care for unaccompanied minors (UAMs) and other children with problems;
- care for other disadvantaged people within the refugee community;
- become more self reliant;
- produce more food for themselves;
- deal effectively with sex related violence problems;
- involve youth more in all activities; and
- maintain privately run pre-schools, primary schools, secondary schools and adult education centres in the camp.

SEKO took over the Refugee Programme, which was formerly run by Diocese of Western Tanganyika Refugee Department

(DWTRD). Since registration it has maintained that programme. Through improved staff and co-operative participation and experience, SEKO is now a partner in all development endeavours.

6. Sources of Funds

Currently, SEKO gets over 85 per cent of its financial support from UNHCR. The rest is sourced from UNICEF, T/FUND-HOLLAND, NWB-Spain and Episcopal Relief and Development based in USA.

7. Capacity Building

Like any other local NGO, SEKO is faced with the problem of building its own capacity including staff training, and exposure to modern technology. However, through UNHCR and Christian Outreach Relief and Development (CORD), in-house training has been possible. More staff training remains imperative so that SEKO is better equipped to handle refugee situations and also be ready to take up challenges of development activities in refugee affected areas when and before the refugees have been repatriated.

8. Future Plans

Plans are underway to introduce a Community Development Programme to the local community within refugee affected areas. A strategic plan has already been adopted. Fundraising, both locally and externally is the next step forward.

SOUTHERN AFRICA EXTENSION UNIT
(SAEU)

Head Office:
P. O Box 70074, Dar es Salaam
Tel: 255 22 2861079-81 Mobile: 0742 602728
Fax: 255 22 2861079
E-mail:saeu@intafrica.com

Contact Person:
Executive Director: Ms. Nderikiyo Elizabeth Ligate
MA Education, University of London, B.A. Makerere University
College, Dip. Ed. Nairobi University College- University of EA.

Kasulu Field Co-ordinator: Mr. Zakayo Msengi
B.A Ed.- UDSM; BA Philosophy - UK.

Kibondo Field Co-ordinator: Mr. Christopher Nkwezi
B.A. UDSM; PG RPL-Dodoma;
PG Admin.-London; Dip. Ed.-Morogoro.

1. Background

SAEU was established in 1984 as an Intergovernmental Organisation under a memorandum of understanding signed by The Government of the United Republic of Tanzania, (GoT); Commonwealth Secretariat, (COMSEC); and the United Nations High Commissioner for Refugees, (UNHCR).

It was reconstituted into an International Non-Governmental Organisation in April 1999. It is a membership organisation with the following categories of members:

- Founder Members;
- Individual members;
- Institutional Members;
- Associate Members; and
- Honorary Members.

2. SAEU's Mission Statement and Vision

The Mission of Southern Africa Extension Unit is to provide sustainable quality products and services in education, relief rehabilitation and community development to as many people as possible in co-operation with other institutions.

SAEU's vision is to become a leading organisation providing affordable quality education, disaster relief and rehabilitation services in sustainable manner through mobilisation of community and in co-operation with other institutions.

3. Organisational Structure

Total number of staff presently employed is 18.

Part time staff: 40 - 50 depending on programme in operation. See the attached chart.

4. Field Experience

In Refugee Education

- Provision of education and training opportunities by Distance Methodology to South African refugees resident in Tanzania, Zambia, Zimbabwe, Botswana, Angola and Uganda 1986 - 1994.

- 1992 - 1996, SAEU established inside South Africa for returnees' education and training programmes. In 1995, SAEU - South Africa was reconstituted to South African Extension Unit Trust run by South Africans. SAEU (Dar Es Salaam) provided technical support until April 1996.
- 1992 - 1994, it operationalised a scholarship project on behalf of an Italian NGO, COSPE.
- From May 1st 2001, SAEU manages Community Services and Education in Mtendeli and Nduta Camps in Kibondo District.
- In Human Resources Development the SAEU has assisted
- Ministries of Education in Dar es Salaam and Zanzibar improve their course modules for in-service Teacher Training Programme (PEP), 1995/1996.
- Ministry of Labour and Youth Development in launching a distance education programme for youth work training 1995/1996.
- In implementing a training programme for all Local Government Councillors in Tanzania Mainland; 1996 - 1997.
- In developing in collaboration with the Open University of Tanzania a Distance Education Certificate Course for Open/Distance Learning Institutions. The certificate course is currently being taught at the Open University of Tanzania's Institute of Continuing Education and is open to students from all over Africa, 1997 - 1998.

5. Main Current Sector Activity

Under Refugee Education

- Implementing a scholarship programme for 245 students located in Secondary Schools, Vocational Colleges, Higher Education Colleges and Universities.
- Implementing a Distance Education programme for refugees in Kigoma region of Tanzania numbering over 800.
- Developing and operationalising 'Ordinary' and 'Advanced' level French course for 300 students in Kigoma region.
- Manages Kibondo field office in Mtendeli and Nduta Refugee Camps in Community Services and Education

Community Services

- Community mobilisation for peace and reconciliation education.
- Tracing unaccompanied minors, adults, and single parents for family reunification and children rights.
- Community Based Rehabilitation (CBR) for the physically and mentally disabled, chronically ill, and elderly.
- Gender mainstreaming and Sexual Gender Based Violence (SGBV). Awareness of SGBV, Assistance to SGBV survivors and women rights.
- Youths, Adolescents, Sports and Culture: Training in reproductive health, HIV/AIDS, healthy and meaningful activities.
- Environment and Friendly Agriculture: Gardening and energy serving techniques.
- Micro projects skills training: Income generating activities and skills training.

Education

- Pre-school;
- Primary school;
- Post Primary (secondary school education); and

Under Human Resource Development

- Development and operationalising courses on the sustenance and promotion of Human Rights for various target groups such as Local Councillors, War Executives, Police Officers, NGOs and CBO's etc.
- Developing and operationalising Science Courses to be taught by the Distance Methodology for private secondary school students in Mbeya region.

6. Other Activities that SAEU is Able to Operate Include

i) Consultancies on:
- Needs assessment surveys; and Research on refugee activities.

ii) Carry out awareness/advocacy/sensitisation programmes for refugees/returnees on:

- Conflict resolution;
- Gender mainstreaming;
- Care of environment;
- Democracy;
- Good Governance;
- Human Rights; and
- Civic and Voter education.

7. Direct Services to Refugees

Phase	Type of Service	Duration	Location
Care and Maintenance	Education Registration/ Record Keeping	From 1984 to 1996	S.A Refugees Resident in Eastern and Southern African Countries.
Repatriation		2 years (1992 -1994)	As above

Type of Service	Location	Donor	Time
Education (DE)	Mtabila Camp	UNHCR	1994 to date
Education Scholarship	In Tanzania educational institutions countrywide	UNHCR	1996 to date

8. Staff Retention

SAEU provides education and training services for new staff and retains established staff in new skills. Also SAEU has a large contingent group of part-time staff which acts as a reservoir for new needs.

9. Sources of Funds

Donor funding by COMSEC, Royal Netherlands Government, Government of Ireland, Commonwealth Local Government

Forum, European Union and Independent Trust of South Africa.

SAEU provides consultancy services and sells its publications.

9.1 Auditing of Financial Reports

SAEU and UNHCR's external auditors audit SAEU's accounts annually.

The SAEU has a five-year corporate plan 2001 - 2006, which is currently in operation.

10. Requirements for Capacity Building

Skills in database, data processing, marketing of services and fund raising.

11. Future Plans

Organise support services for Open University students (refugees and non Refugees) Start Health and Nutrition Education classes in the areas of disease prevention e.g. Heart cancer, arthritis, headaches, asthma etc.

SAEU'S ORGANISATIONAL STRUCTURE

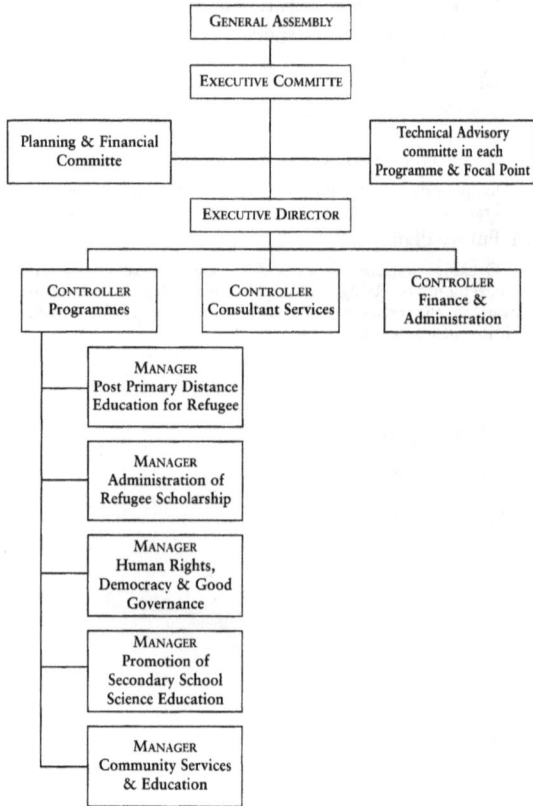

```
                    GENERAL ASSEMBLY

                    EXECUTIVE COMMITTE

Planning & Financial                    Technical Advisory
    Committe                            committe in each
                                    Programme & Focal Point

                    EXECUTIVE DIRECTOR

   CONTROLLER          CONTROLLER          CONTROLLER
   Programmes       Consultant Services    Finance &
                                          Administration

              MANAGER
          Post Primary Distance
          Education for Refugee

              MANAGER
          Administration of
          Refugee Scholarship

              MANAGER
          Human Rights,
          Democracy & Good
          Governance

              MANAGER
          Promotion of
          Secondary School
          Science Education

              MANAGER
          Community Services
          & Education
```

TANZANIA RED CROSS SOCIETY (TRCS)

Address:
P.O. Box 1133, DAR ES SALAAM

Contact Person:
Alhaji A.O. Kimbisa
MA (Business Administration):
Secretary General.

1. Background

Tanzania Red Cross Society (TRCS) was established through an act of Parliament in 1962. The Society was recognised as a National Society and admitted into the International Red Cross organs in 1962 after Tanzania signed the relevant Geneva conventions on December 12th, 1962. Additional protocols were signed on February 15th, 1983. TRCS is part of the world wide Red Cross Movement, which has incorporated 171 National Red Cross and Red Crescent Societies.

2. Mission Statement

To alleviate all forms of suffering without discrimination as to race, nationality, ideology or religious belief. It is guided by seven fundamental principles which are:

- humanity;
- impartiality;
- neutrality;
- independence;
- universality;
- voluntary service; and
- unity.

3. Organisational Structure

The organisation comprises Red Cross Volunteers registered in grass root branches. Permanent staff and temporary staff depending on the nature of the operation needs manage daily activities.

4. Field Experience

The organisation is relief and development oriented with wide experiences in relief and development programmes, as will be illustrated bellow.

4.1 Refugee Programmes

TRCS and the local community in Ngara assisted the first batch of Burundi refugees in the 1993 wave before other organisations joined.

TRCS initiated the establishment of some refugee camps such as Lukole Camp in Ngara and Lugufu Camp in Kigoma.

In 1994, during the Rwanda genocide, TRCS worked in collaboration with International Federation of the Red Cross and Red Crescent (IFRC) in camp management at Benaco and Lukole Camps with the populations of 500,000 (Rwandese) and 40,000 (Burundians) respectively. Other services offered to the operation were health, water and sanitation; tracing and warehousing.

In 1997, after the mass repatriation of Rwandese, TRCS was assigned the camp management services by UNHCR where it rendered food and non-food items distribution to the 150,000 Burundi refugees at Lukole. Others were construction of camp infrastructures, road repairs and maintenance, Camp lament - plot demarcation and allocation and camp profile.

To support the activities above, TRCS has the Relief Camp Department, Finance and Administration Department, Logistics Department and Security Department, all under the Team Leader.

In the development project in Ngara, TRCS conducts campaigns against the HIV/AIDS and offers services like home-based care, education and awareness to those affected or their families, and the rehabilitation of the environment involving the local community.

After the repartition TRCS also continues with the family unification across the borders. In the absence of the international organisations TRCS offers health services, operates water programmes and warehousing/logistics from experience gained from the IFRC.

Kigoma Operation

The TRCS Kigoma refugee programme commenced in 1996. It currently caters for 96,000 Burundians based in Mtabila I, II and Muyovozi. An additional caseload of Congolese refugees was also added in 1997. The current caseload (population) is 73,000 Congolese refugees based in Lugufu I and II. Tanzania Red Cross provides health and water and sanitation services to four camps of

Lugufu, Mtabila I & II and Muyovozi. It also provides camp management services to Muyovozi and Lugufu Camps.

Local Community Programmes

- The society has a health department, which focuses on HIV/AIDS Programmes. It co-ordinates various activities including:
  - Support of teaching about HIV/AIDS in primary schools in Rukwa, Kagera and Kilimanjaro regions;
  - Home based care and social support to affected families;
  - Training of Traditional Birth Attendants (TBAs); and
  - Support to disadvantaged orphans in 19 primary schools.
- The department also deals with Primary Health Care Programmes in Mwanza, Dar es Salaam, Masasi and Zanzibar.
- It co-ordinates Reproductive Health programmes for 38 villages in Kigoma; water and sanitation for 5 villages in Kigoma, other beneficiaries of water and sanitation for Dar Es Salaam and Zanzibar.
- Youth family life education programme involves the out-of-school youths and focuses on improving health among them and increased health care and social support at community level.

5. Other Activities

- first aid training;
- blood donor recruitment;
- training; and
- dissemination of international humanitarian laws.

6. Staff Retention

Most activities are performed on a voluntary basis. Volunteers are the backbone of the National Society and most of them are retained in accordance with the Volunteers' Management Policy.

41

7. Sources of Funds

For the refugee programmes, UNHCR, ICRC, FRC, DFID and other participating National Societies fund TRCS. For the local community programmes UNICEF, British Red Cross, American Red Cross, ICRC, CARE-Tanzania, Swedish Red Cross, Norwegian Embassy and USAID fund TRCS.

8. Evaluation

Most of TRCS programmes are evaluated annually and reports are shared with potential donors.

9. Requirements for Capacity Building

TRCS still needs more training on fund raising project proposal and report writing.

10. Future Plans

TRCS intends to put more emphasis on local community based programmes through Red Cross branches.

11. Strength of the Organisation

TRCS has well organised structure, potential of skilled, experienced manpower and dedicated volunteers throughout the country.

TRCS ORGANISATIONAL STUCTURE

GENERAL ASSEMBLY

NATIONAL
MANAGEMENT
COMMITTE

SECRETARY GENERAL

DEPUTY SECRETARY
GENERAL

| DIRECTOR INFORMATION & TRACING | DIRECTOR OF FIELD OPERATION | DIRECTOR OF FINANCE & ADMINSTRATION | HEALTH COORDINATOR |

| | | | HIV | FIRST AID | BLOOD DONOR | WATER/ SANITATION |

| DISASTER RESPONSE PROGRAMME | DISASTER PREPAREDNESS | BRANCH DEVELOPMENT | | SOLID WASTE PROGRAMME |

REFUGES
RELIEF
OPERATIONS

KIGOMA   NGARA

| HEALTH | RELIEF | FINANCE & ADMIN. | LOGISTICS | RELIEF | FINANCE & ADMIN. | LOGISTICS |

| WATER SANITATION | CAMP MANAGER | SECURITY | | | SECURITY |

43

TANZANIA WATER AND ENVIRONMENTAL SANITATION (TWESA)

Head Office Address:
Sekei Area, Incofin Building P. O. Box 741, ARUSHA,
Tel./Fax (027) 2506454,
E-mail: twesa@habari.co.tz

Contact Persons:
Chairperson: Bigambo Nandiga
BSc (Eng.) - MSc, Civil (Eng.) - Watsan Programme officer:
Haidari Kassim, BSc - Civil (Eng.)

1. Status and Background

TWESA is a non-profit and non-political NGO. It was registered under the Societies Ordinance (CAP) 337 as an NGO on 30th June 1997 and issued with Registration Certificate No. So. 9090.

The establishment of TWESA was the result of perceived need among Tanzanians with experience working in emergencies, and through, support from Oxfam (GB) Tanzania Office, to build local capacity to respond to emergencies and development needs.

2. TWESA's Mission Statement and Vision

To relieve suffering of victims in emergencies and of poor communities in needy areas, through development and implementation of improved and protected water supply and environmental sanitation.

TWESA envisages communities free from water and sanitation - related diseases and hardships.

3. TWESA's Membership and Organisational Structure

3.1 The Constitution

TWESA's activities are governed by its constitution under which there are three principle organs in charge of TWESA's day-to-day activities. They are: the General Assembly, the Executive Committee and the Secretariat.

The General Assembly is made up of all registered members of TWESA. It meets once bi-annually and it is the supreme decision making body on all matters pertaining to rights and duties of the members and of organs of TWESA.

The Executive Committee is responsible for planning, administering and regulating the management of TWESA. It consists of: the Chairperson, Secretary, Treasurer who are also referred to as office bearers and three other TEC members.

The day-to-day management of TWESA's activities and implementation of projects are entrusted to the Secretariat headed by the Co-ordinator who is also Secretary to the Executive

Committee. Other members of the secretariat are the Administrator and Programme Officers.

3.2 Membership

TWESA is a membership organisation with four categories of membership, namely; founder, ordinary, corporate and honorary members.

Membership is open to any resident of Tanzania who is a beneficiary of at least one of TWESA's programmes, is involved in TWESA's activities or is a member of an organisation or institution whose objectives are similar to those under TWESA constitution.

3.3 Total Number of Staff

- Full-time staff: three; Co-ordinator, Programme Officer and Administrator.
- Project staff: Their number depends on a specific project, currently there are 50 staff members stationed at Kibondo and Kasulu field offices.
- Other staff: TWESA maintains a database of its members and personnel with experience in emergencies. This group acts as a contingent workforce for easy deployment as and when need arises.

4. Major Programmes

- Humanitarian Assistance (Refugees' water supply and sanitation)
- Rural and small towns water supply and sanitation systems development and/or improvement
- Consultancy services for designing, construction supervision and management of water supply and sanitation programmes, particularly in rural areas and small towns.

5. Field Experience

5.1 Refugee Assistance

- Since 1998, following the successful teaming up and take over from Oxfam, TWESA has, for about 4 years, been efficiently operating water supply and sanitation facilities for 50,000 Burundian refugees in Nduta camp, Kibondo district, Kigoma region.

- Recently, TWESA has signed another tripartite agreement with UNHCR and the Ministry of Home Affairs (MHA) authorising TWESA to carry out, from January 2002, the operation and maintenance of water supply and sanitation facilities for Congolese refugees in Nyarugusu camp, Kasulu district, Kigoma region.

5.2 Rural Water Supply and Sanitation

- In the years 1999 to 2002 TWESA successfully implemented water supply and sanitation programmes in the refugee affected areas, which now serves over 40,000 people in 9 villages of Kibondo district.
- In 1999 and early 2000, TWESA participated in a UNHCR funded emergency programme of construction of spring water sources in 4 villages of Kibondo district which are refugee entry points along the border with Burundi.

5.3 Consultancy Works

- TWESA was involved in consultancy works for preparation of proposals and fund raising activities for water supply and sanitation projects in Kasulu, Ngara and Karagwe districts' refugee affected areas; Shinyanga urban water supply, Singida urban water supply, Igunga town water supply and Bukwaya area in Musoma district.

6. Sources of Fund

- Main sources of TWESA funds include the following:
- Grants from donors for project implementation: major donors include Oxfam GB, UNHCR, UNICEF and Oxfam Ireland.
- Sale of service: TWESA provides consultancy services for preparations of project proposals for the implementation and management of water supply and environmental sanitation programmes.

- Members' contributions: TWESA members do make annual subscriptions as part of their constitutional obligation.

7. Future Plans and Challenges ahead

The main areas where TWESA strives to excel so as to meet its goals more effectively and efficiently are:

- Organisational capacity building;
- Negotiation skills for fund raising and availability of fully funded projects (contracts); and
- Management of rural and small towns water supply and sanitation.

TWESA ORGANISATIONAL STUCTURE

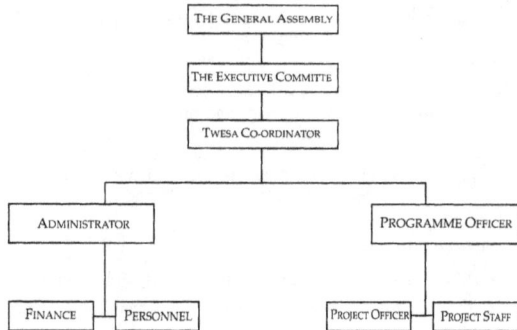

```
            ┌──────────────────────────┐
            │  THE GENERAL ASSEMBLY     │
            └──────────────────────────┘
                        │
            ┌──────────────────────────┐
            │  THE EXECUTIVE COMMITTE   │
            └──────────────────────────┘
                        │
            ┌──────────────────────────┐
            │  TWESA CO-ORDINATOR       │
            └──────────────────────────┘
                        │
         ┌──────────────┴────────────────────────┐
  ┌────────────────┐                     ┌──────────────────────┐
  │ ADMINISTRATOR  │                     │  PROGRAMME OFFICER    │
  └────────────────┘                     └──────────────────────┘
         │                                          │
  ┌──────────┬──────────┐              ┌──────────────┬──────────────┐
  │ FINANCE  │ PERSONNEL│              │ PROJECT OFFICER│ PROJECT STAFF│
  └──────────┴──────────┘              └──────────────┴──────────────┘
```

CHAMA CHA UZAZI NA MALEZI BORA
TANZANIA
(UMATI)

Address:
Samora/Zanaki Street
P.O. Box 1372, Dar es Salaam
Tel: 255-22-2117774/2111639, Fax: 255-22-2139050
Email: umati@africaonline.co.tz

Contact Person:
Walter Mbunda
B.A. (Stat.), M.B. (Dem.)- Executive Director

1. Background

UMATI was established in 1959 and officially registered in 1960 as a non-governmental organisation. It is a national, non-political, non-profit organisation specialised in the provision of Reproductive Health Services through the following approaches.

1.1 Facility (or clinic) Based

The association provides comprehensive sexual and reproductive health services in clinics located in different regions. Also under this are Youth Centres, which provide recreational, library and clinic services.

1.2 Community Services, International Relations and Membership

These entail mobilising the community to appoint individuals who are trained to provide counselling and teach proper use of contraceptives to fellow community members.

UMATI is a member of the International Planned Parenthood Federation (IPPF), which has its headquarters in London, U.K.

UMATI is a membership organisation with the following categories of members:

- Ordinary Members;
- Life Members;
- Honorary Members; and
- Corporate Members.

UMATI membership is open to Tanzanians from age 10, who believe in and accept its vision, mission and values.

2. UMATI's Vision

UMATI envisages a society where all people, especially the young, have the right to and enjoy quality sexual and reproductive health.

2.1 Mission Statement

UMATI is an autonomous, national non-profit, non-political and national NGO that will:

- commit itself to the youth as the primary client for advocacy on SRH rights and the elimination of harmful practices to enable them make free and informed choices about their sexual life and well-being.

- provide leadership and play a catalytic role in the provision of quality model youth friendly services that are market oriented, gender sensitive and with a special focus on the prevention and management of STIs, HIV/AIDS as well as unwanted pregnancies.

- maximise the use of the network of experienced volunteers, staff and well-established institutional structures that are based on a sustainable resource base.

2.2 The New Paradigm

Sexual and Reproductive Health, which incorporates Family Planning as one key component, is the new paradigm of UMATI.

2.3 Priority Components

Within the SRH framework priority components are:

- Prevention of STI/HIV/AIDS;
- Prevention of unwanted pregnancies;
- Elimination of harmful practices;
- Prevention of unsafe abortion;
- Promotion of good behaviour in human sexuality; and
- Prevention of substance abuse.

2.4 Key Goal Areas

- Advocacy
- Service delivery
- Resource mobilisation
- Research and Marketing
- Institutional/Management capacity strengthening

3. Organisational Structure

UMATI is governed by volunteers through the Annual General Meeting (AGM). UMATI operates through the National Council and Executive Committee on its day-to-day policy issues. It is a national NGO with similar structures reflected at regional and district levels. The day-to-day management of UMATI is provided by the Executive Director (ED), who is assisted by three directorates, namely Programmes, Finance and Administration and Research and Marketing. (See the Organisational Structure attached).

4. Field Experience

1960 - 1974: UMATI was sole provider of information, advocacy, and Family planning (FP) services.

1974 - 1984: FP being provided in Maternal Child Health (MCH) setting UMATI roles are defined as:

i. creating awareness on and advocate for the Importance of FP to the health of mother, child and father;

ii. training all health service providers from the government and private agencies on how to provide FP services; and

iii. procuring and distributing materials including contraceptives and equipment for FP throughout the country.

In 1989 the government founded the national Family Planning Programme, which among others pledged to undertake all the activities UMATI was undertaking. In the light of the result of the 1988 National Census results and the 1992 Demographic Health Survey (DHS), UMATI made a 1992 -1996 strategic plan decides to refocus the services as follows:

Community Based Services entail mobilising communities to appoint individuals who are then trained to provide counselling about contraceptives to fellow community members. Community based service activities include:

• Integrated projects (IP) are set up after identification of community felt needs. UMATI has several such projects that have proved successful, e.g. the De-worming/Family Planning; Income Generating /Family Planning in Swansea, Mooch, Dar es Salaam and Morogoro.

• Youth Centres provide meeting places for recreational, information/ counselling and clinical services for youth thus creating chances for Sexual and Reproductive Health education and services.

• Young Men As Equal partners Projects (YMEP) aim at promoting male involvement and leadership in SRH matters.

From experience gathered over the 40 years of its existence UMATI is able to mobilise the general public for health and other related campaigns; provide training in sexual and reproductive health for institutions and individuals; conducts (operational) researches; train in quality SRH control; design Information, Education, Communication (IEC) materials; and provide emergency relief operations.

5. Experience in Direct Services to Refugees

Following the political turmoil in Burundi and Rwanda in 1993 and 1994 respectively, UMATI with AMREF established Reproductive Health Services in Ngara to serve over 500,000 refugees settled in 4 camps. UMATI's responsibilities were to:

- train Reproductive Health Services providers;
- provide information and counselling to refugees;
- produce and distribute contraceptives;
- provide various services including health, nutrition, community services education and environmental education; and
- supervise Reproductive Health Services in clinics, which by then were being managed by different NGOs.

These services were extended to Karagwe Refugee Programme in 1995.

In 1996, UMATI included General Health and Nutrition services in the two camps of Kagenyi and Rubwera in Karagwe District, which had a total of 40,000 refugees.

In the same year UMATI was involved in repatriating 120,000Rwandan refugees from Karagwe camps.

Following the repatriation, between 1997 and 1998, UMATI was involved in the refugee-affected communities that surrounded the camp by integrating the refugee health services in the local health structure.

UMATI joined the Kigoma Refugee Programme in March 1998 by teaming up with International Red Cross (IRC) and later taking over the management of health and nutrition; and community services and environment at Kanembwa and Mkugwa camps, in Kibondo District. In January 1999, Education Services in Mkungwa were handed over to UMATI by TRCS, and the SGBV Programme by International Rescue Committee (IRC) at Kanembwa and Mkungwa in December of the same year.

In late 1999, UMATI started to establish and manage Community and Education Services in the new camp of Karago.

UMATI's experiences are summarised in the following table:

Phase	Type of Service	Duration and Site
Influx Emergency	Community Services & Education	Few weeks in Karago
Care and Maintenance	Community Services, Education and Environment	1999-2000 in Karago
	Health and Nutrition, Community Services, Education Environment and Sexual and Gender Based Violence (SGBV)	1994 to-date in Ngara, Karagwe and Kibondo
Repatriation	Health Services	3 weeks (1996)
Advocacy	Nil	Nil

6. Future Plans

UMATI intends to retain its capacity to provide services in emergency situations. This will be achieved by ensuring that after the repatriations, there will be activities among the local communities around the former refugee camps.

7. Sources of Fund

UMATI has a number of donors to its regular Projects. IPPF provides the bigger share of UMATI's budget. Other donors include Pathfinder International, USAID, SIDA, CIDA, JICA, JOICFP, RFSU, and the Bill Gates Foundation. The Refugee Project is funded mainly by UNHCR (about 80 per cent).

7.1 Initiatives to Generate More Funds

Apart from external donors, UMATI makes efforts to generate its operational funds from local donors by providing consultancy works to other institutions.

8. Requirements for Capacity Building

Establishment of a department dealing with Emergence within UMATI's structure, which will be responsible in writing proposals for submission to different donors to address any emerging issue.

ORGANISATIONAL STUCTURE
Chama cha Uzazi na Malezi bora Tanzania (UMATI)

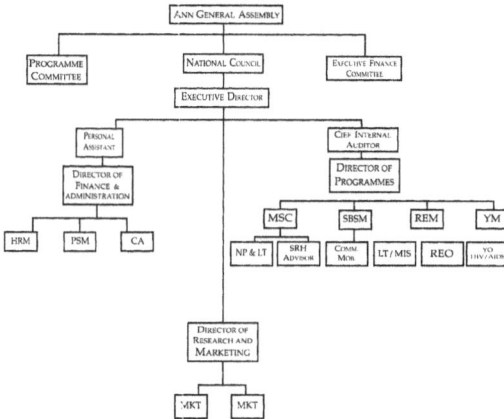

KEY OF ABBREVIATIONS:

MKT	-	Marketing
DRMA	-	Director of Research and Marketing
CBSM	-	Community Based Services Manager
REM	-	Research and Evaluation Manager
NP&LT	-	National Permanent and Long-term
SRH	-	Sexual Reproductive Health
COMM.		
MOB.	-	Community Mobilisation
IT	-	Information Technology
MIS	-	Management Information System
REO	-	Research and Evaluation officer
YO	-	Youth officer
HIV/AIDS	-	Human Immune Virus/ Acquired Immune Deficiency Syndrome
YO CNT	-	Youth Officer - Centres

WORLD VISION TANZANIA (WVT)

Address:
P.O. Box 6070, Arusha
Tel. 255 27 2508820/2504479, Fax: 255 27 2508248
E-mail: Tanzania@wvi.org

Contact Persons:

At national level: Mr. George Mkanza
National Direcor

At field level: Mr. Inyami Sengasenga
Team Leader-Kasulu Programmes

61

1. Background

World Vision Tanzania is a non-profit organisation established in 1981. It is a relief and development organisation which has overall goal of promoting human development and especially to meet the need of children. (Bringing hope to the children of Tanzania).

2. Mission Statement

To follow our Lord and Saviour Jesus Christ in working with the poor and oppressed, to promote human transformation, seek justice and bear witness to the good news of the Kingdom of God.

- The Mission is achieved through integrated, holistic commitment to:
- Transformational development, that is community based and sustainable focus especially on the needs of children.
- Emergency relief that assists people afflicted by conflict or disaster.
- Promotion of justice that seeks to change unjust structures affecting the poor among whom WVT work.
- Strategic initiatives that serve the church in the fulfilment of its mission.
- Public awareness that leads to informed understanding, giving involvement and prayer.
- Witness to Jesus Christ by life, deed, word and sign that encourages people to respond to the gospel.

3. Organisational Structure

World Vision Tanzania is governed by a local Board of Trustees and is registered under the Trustees Incorporation Ordinance. The National Director is assisted by four division Directors of Organisation. The Board of Trustees appoints Board members for a term of three years renewable. The National Director is also appointed by the Board, and is one of the Board members. The line of communication between the policy makers(Board of Trustees) and the executive staff (Directors of the Division) is through the National Director).

4. Areas of Operation

The Head Office of World Vision-Tanzania is based in Arusha. In keeping with the policy of decentralisation, the organisation has 5 zones with 88 development and 1 relief projects which are located in 23 districts of the country. The zones include:

- Northern Zone: covering Arusha and Kilimanjaro Regions.
- Central Zone: covering Dodoma and Singida Regions.
- Lake Zone: covering Shinyanga and Tabora Regions.
- Kagera Zone : covering Kagera region.
- Eastern Zone: covering Tanga, Morogoro and Dar es Salaam Regions.

There is also Kasulu Programmes zone that covers Kasulu District.

4.1 Development Projects:

The types of projects are standard community based programmes calle Area Development programme (ADP) which cover population between 20,000 to 100,000 people. Total beneficiaries are estimated to be over 3 million Tanzanians.

Main sector interventions facilitated by World Vision Tanzania in the ADPs are Agriculture and Livestock, Health, Primary Education, Environment, clean and safe water, Environment, Christian Witness and income generating activities (IGAS).

4.2 Relief Projects:

World Vision Tanzania is doing camp management in Nyarugusu Camp. The targeted beneficiaries are around 55,000 Congolese refugees. WVT has been dong this assignment since November 1996.

5. Staff Retention

To ensure that World Vision Tanzania does not lose staff and her people become jobless especially when refugee project closes, it has started to initiate development projects. Kasulu Survival Programme has started its second phase since July 2002 and at the same time proposal are under way to establish ADP in the area.

6. Sources of Funds

WVT depends on the following sources:

- Donation from partnership offices being child sponsorship or grand donation.
- Local funs raised in Tanzania by the National Resource Development office in Dar es Salaam.

7. Requirements for Capacity Building

- Disaster Mitigation
- Information Technology

8. Auditing

WVT has an Internal Audit Unit that is doing Developmental Audit to every project at least once per two years.

WVT is also audited by External Auditors on an annual basis. Also partnership offices do audit WVT programmes.

www.ingramcontent.com/pod-product-compliance
Lightning Source LLC
Chambersburg PA
CBHW021824270326
41932CB00007B/322